God Is...

God Is...

A 30 Day Devotional of Spiritual Metaphors and Sanctified Adverbs

Robin Zaruba

IE Works
Kingwood, TX

Copyright © 2015 Robin Zaruba

All rights reserved. No part of this publication may be reproduced, distributed, or transmitted in any form or by any means, including photocopying, recording, or other electronic or mechanical methods, without the prior written permission of the author, except in the case of brief quotations embodied in critical reviews and certain other noncommercial uses permitted by copyright law. For permission requests, write to the author at the address below.

Robin Zaruba, 3810 Babbling Creek Drive, Kingwood TX 77345

Cover design by Angela Brans

Scripture quotations are from the ESV® Bible (The Holy Bible, English Standard Version®), copyright © 2001 by Crossway, a publishing ministry of Good News Publishers. Used by permission. All rights reserved.

Scripture taken from the Holy Bible, NEW INTERNATIONAL VERSION®, NIV® Copyright © 1973, 1978, 1984, 2011 by Biblica, Inc.®Used by permission. All rights reserved worldwide.

Scripture quotations taken from the Amplified® Bible, Copyright © 1954, 1958, 1962, 1964, 1965, 1987 by The Lockman Foundation. Used by permission. (www.Lockman.org)

Scripture taken from the NEW AMERICAN STANDARD BIBLE®, Copyright © 1960,1962,1963,1968,1971,1972,1973,1975,1977,1995 by The Lockman Foundation. Used by permission.

New Living Translation (NLT) Holy Bible. New Living Translation copyright © 1996 by Tyndale Charitable Trust. Used by permission of Tyndale House Publishers.

Scripture taken from the New King James Version. Copyright © 1982 by Thomas Nelson, Inc. Used by permission. All rights reserved.

The Living Bible copyright © 1971 by Tyndale House Foundation. Used by permission of Tyndale House Publishers Inc., Carol Stream, Illinois 60188. All rights reserved. The Living Bible, TLB, and the The Living Bible logo are registered trademarks of Tyndale House Publishers.

Scripture quotations marked (CEV) are from the Contemporary English Version Copyright © 1991, 1992, 1995 by American Bible Society, Used by Permission.

Contents

Endorsements	xi
Acknowledgements	xiv
Dedication	xvi
Foreword	xvii
Preface	xviii
Introduction	1
1. Day 1: God is… Light	5
2. Day 2: God is… Just In Time	8
3. Day 3: God is… Turner Of Tides	11
4. Day 4: God Is… Treasure Hunter	14
5. Day 5: God is… Now and Not Yet	17
6. Day 6: God Is… Thirst Quencher	20
7. Day 7: God Is… Not Surprised	23
8. Day 8: God Is… Home Sweet Home	26

9.	Day 9: God Is… Once And For All	*29*
10.	Day 10: God is… My Nightlight	*32*
11.	Day 11: God Is…No Regrets	*35*
12.	Day 12: God is… Singer Over Me	*38*
13.	Day 13: God Is… Dream Granter	*41*
14.	Day 14: God Is… Storm Calmer	*44*
15.	Day 15: God Is… Gift Giver	*48*
16.	Day 16: God Is… Good All the Time	*51*
17.	Day 17: God Is… Burden Lifter	*54*
18.	Day 18: God Is… Closer than a Brother	*57*
19.	Day 19: God Is… New Every Morning	*61*
20.	Day 20: God Is… Pursuer	*64*
21.	Day 21: God Is… Extravagant	*67*
22.	Day 22: God Is… Liberator	*71*
23.	Day 23: God is… Good News	*74*
24.	Day 24: God Is… Unseen	*77*
25.	Day 25: God Is… In Control	*81*
26.	Day 26: God Is… Nevertheless	*85*
27.	Day 27: God Is… Not If, but When	*89*

28.	Day 28: God Is… Listener	*92*
29.	Day 29: God Is… The Greatest Story Ever Told	*95*
30.	Day 30: God is… Not Me (and for that I am grateful)	*98*
	Epilogue	*103*
	Appendix	*104*

Endorsements

I have read dozens of devotionals through the years. Of the ones written by a worship leader, this is by far the most thoughtful, insightful and profitable. Robin captures a lot of what the typical person senses to be true about God and life, and what they long for in their pursuit to know Him. With poetic eloquence like only a worship leader can do, Robin guides you through his life experience in a way that will enrich your world and give you a renewed passion to pursue God. By giving us a thoughtful glance through his life lens, Robin assures us that this common ground we tread is good, thus making our steps lighter and more meaningful in our pursuit of knowing Christ. This is more than just a worthwhile read. I find myself connecting on a personal level and quoting his thoughts and prose to friends!

Mike Harder – Author & Executive Pastor, Liberti Church, Philadelphia www.libertichurch.org

As a counselor, I am drawn to writing that encourages and empowers rather than words that elicit guilt and discouragement.

ENDORSEMENTS

Robin has managed a wonderful balance in leading people to take positive action (what they have control of) while at the same time trusting in God's grace and timing. Reflecting on the daily writing causes me to know I can handle whatever life brings my way because "God Is…" beside me, leading me, supporting me in just the way I need today. I appreciate metaphors which, like good stories, invite us in. The citing of literature and films helps people in this contemporary culture make connections to the scripture, the primary source of inspiration.

Jerry L. Terrill, Ph.D.

I am really excited for my friend and brother in Christ, Robin Zaruba. I have known Robin for many years as a very skilled musician, singer, and songwriter. Now I find there's another gifting inside of him that takes his ministry to a completely different level of maturity. Robin's 30 day devotional is filled with "right now" life applications to which everyone can relate. I love it! The Word of God is truly the Bread of life! I highly recommend his devotional to all people saved and unsaved. There are nuggets of gold in each day that will encourage, comfort and build up each one's faith in a deeper relationship with Jesus Christ.

David Huff – singer, songwriter, and leader of the Dove Award nominated Christian band "David and the Giants" www.davidhuff.com

Robin Zaruba's wit and lucid wisdom always pepper our weekly

staff meetings. In this devotional, you will enjoy that same 'Robinesque' insight for living.

Dr. D. M. Woodward – Senior Pastor, Kingwood Bible Church, Kingwood TX www.kingwoodbiblechurch.com

I've read devotionals that seem to be leading me through daily chores, but Robin is a songwriter and a worship leader whose book takes my heart on a journey into the presence of God. I read, and I'm taught who God is from His Word and how that relates to who I am. It connects me to who God wants me to be. So "God Is…" isn't just another daily devotional where I check off my list of 'to-do's.' It's a refreshing spiritual journey. And I thirst for more of who God is.

J. Chad Barrett – Connection Pastor, Kingwood Bible Church, and Author of "Journey to Freedom: The Pursuit of Authentic Fellowship among Men" www.ieworks.org

Acknowledgements

This devotional would not have been possible without the help of Cherry Smith. She and her husband Robert provided me their lake house cost-free for several days in which to finish the bulk of this work that I had been sitting on for over a year. I have known them since I was a teenager. Of all the people in my life, Cherry has extended grace to me when it was certainly not deserved; mercy when I should have received condemnation; and love when no one would have questioned judgment. Cherry, when I think of the grace of God, I think of you.

Danielle: You love me so much. I have been loud when you would have me quiet. I have been annoyingly forward when you would have me more restrained. I feel I lack so much of what you need, but you love me still. Thank you for putting up with me and showing me how to change one day at a time.

For my kids: One day I will not be here. Lord knows my

ACKNOWLEDGEMENTS

own father's passing came upon us unexpectedly, in the worst way. My hope is that when my final day comes you will be able to crack open the pages of this book to hear my voice and feel God and me watching over you. I love you.

Loving thanks to my mom and brother for teaching me the value of good storytelling, giving me a wealth of life stories, and helping me have the courage to learn from them.

To my editors: Chad Barrett, Stephen Zaruba, and Tim Smith. Your insights challenged me and made this work even more rewarding.

Finally, to Cyndy Mathis: thank you for encouraging me that some initial scribbles on my iPhone could be turned into a book.

Dedication

For my late father.
You taught me many things about God
even when you did not know it
and I was not listening.
I love you, and I can't wait to see you again.

Foreword

I love creative thinkers – people who make me think outside the mundane point of view the world has a way of leading me into, and helping me peer into the massive creative heart of our God. Robin Zaruba does just that in this new devotional, *God Is... a 30 Day Devotional of Spiritual Metaphors and Sanctified Adverbs*. I would encourage anyone who loves and recognizes the power of Words – THE Word – to dive into this beautifully written book. While easy to read, it is simultaneously thought provoking and encouraging. I love it!

Dennis Jernigan – worship leader, author of the song *You Are My All in All* and the autobiography, *Sing Over Me* www.dennisjernigan.com

Preface

When I was initially inspired to begin this devotional, I sensed a tinge of elation, quickly followed by a deep pessimism. I felt a bit like Admiral James Stockdale, the 1992 3rd party vice presidential candidate, who famously exclaimed in his first televised debate, "Who am I? Why am I here?" Or, to paraphrase the psalmist, "Who am I, Lord, that thou art mindful of me?" I am just a man who hopes to share some wisdom he has picked up along the journey. I am a worship leader, and worship leaders are encouragers.

Now, a devotional should stir the heart, not just inform the head. And part of that experience is reading or hearing something in a way you might not have heard or considered before. I hope this book takes you on a journey of what you thought you knew, around twists and turns of life and faith, to arrive at a fresh understanding of God. But remember: God is who he is, not who we would have him be. I seek to illuminate, to peal back. Not to invent things, but to help reveal them.

In L. Frank Baum's *The Wizard of Oz,* Dorothy crosses

the threshold from dull black and white into Technicolor brilliance:

"*Dorothy sat up and noticed that the house was not moving; nor was it dark, for the bright sunshine came in at the window, flooding the little room. She sprang from her bed and with Toto at her heels ran and opened the door. The little girl gave a cry of amazement and looked about her, her eyes growing bigger and bigger at the wonderful sights she saw.*"

My prayer is that you would cross that threshold; that you might see God with fresh eyes, in a way that rightly reflects the magnitude of what he has done for you and how he loves you completely. Take a deep breath and step on through.

– Robin Zaruba

Introduction

I have to be honest. My first thought when asked to contribute an introduction to this book by Robin was, "Sure, the Church of Christ in the 21st century needs another devotional - NOT!" Frankly, my fear is not that the church of the 21st century has not had enough devotion, but rather that the church of the 21st century has not had enough demotion. *Brokenness. Humility. Servanthood. Placing the needs of others above their own needs.* The church can often times seem more vested in its own success as an organization than in the personal growth and success of the people they have been called to serve.

And then I thought, *wait, Robin is all about service to others through his ministry of music, song, worship, and Christ-filled living"*, and so I conceded and agreed to write an introduction for this book and add some insights into the man we call Robin. So here are my thoughts on this very lofty and unique subject.

When I look at devotionals in a Christian bookstore, I consider two things primarily. First: *Does the author know God intimately and do they live out of the truth in the Bible?* And Second: *Does the author serve Christ with reckless abandon, no holds barred, no reserve for self or stockpile of benefits for personal gain?* OK, I lied, I have a third. Does the author connect to me on a personal level? That is to say, do they write to some generic and undisclosed reader or do they address me where I am living at the moment?

First, I have absolutely no doubt that Robin walks closely with God. I witnessed it for the years we served together in suburban Philadelphia. And even more telling was the reality that when I conducted our monthly all staff meetings, I included a fun game testing Bible knowledge. The staff soon learned it was wise to sit with Robin since he always out-gunned the other members of the 51 member team with his stunning recall of Bible information, Bible trivia, and Bible history. **This man Robin, he knows his Bible.**

Second, I watched Robin stand for truth, passion for his ministry call, and integrity with his ministry vision, even when it cost him unpopularity, argument, and the occasional "boo-hiss" among his peers and some late adapter congregants. Never did I see Robin hide or reverse his conviction because the road to actualizing his vision was going to be hard and painful. **This man Robin, he can be counted on.**

Third, Robin lives real life, not the camouflage of a life hidden behind Bible verse, Spiritual catch phrase, or blame shifting. Robin owns his life – and I mean he owns it completely, taking responsibility for his flaws and all. I

INTRODUCTION

watched him closely as he lived with transparency and vulnerability. His life was Christ inspired and God supported and Spirit guided. I watched Robin walk through some tough waters – both professionally and personally. *This man Robin, he walks the talk.*

SO, if this man Robin can do the hard things I've mentioned, you would be wise to read, absorb, and glean from his writing. I know with confidence you will uncover things that will help refine, inspire, and challenge you to excellence in your faith.

Only one warning: if you ever share Robin's presence, prepare yourself for periods of uncontrolled smiling. *This man Robin, he knows how to enjoy life.*

Enjoy this book, and more, enjoy the Christ revealed here.

- chuck faber, Consultant Pastor to Northeast Presbyterian Church, Columbia, SC

1

Day 1: God is... Light

When the darkness is scratching, biting, clawing
   And shrieking its way to consuming me
   And I am pleading, begging, aching to get out of *me*
   The place where the darkness wants to invade…

   At that moment God Is Light arrives
   Having set out the moment my cry arose
   Like Archangel Michael beating back the Dark Prince

   Except this is not like Mike. This is God Is Light
   This is the Radiant One
   This is He who answers when called
   And His light sends the darkness screeching
   First sideways then headlong
   Skittering like a hard-thrown stone on a placid water top

And finally, in its own outer darkness, scolded and rebuked
Darkness licks its wounds and plots a return
Knowing that next time the arrow's aim
    will not be so nearly true
He will be back, but he will know
    with whose child he contends
This child has a protector and God is Light is his name

2 Samuel 22:29 (NIV) "You are my lamp, O Lord; the Lord turns my darkness into light."

The Way I See It...

The Bible is a very poor rulebook. As rulebooks go, it is merciless in its standard. Thou shalt NOT. However, as a lifebook, it is full of hope, promise, and healing. That is as it should be, for it is our inability to follow God's perfect law that points us to Christ, our Lord of Last Resort.

As I told a friend once, "The Bible is not just the story of what should be [i.e. moral rules], but of what was, what is, and what is to come." When I search his word and pray God lights my path. Not a path that leads to rules and death, but one that winds to mercy and life. I'd like to fully know the mystery of how that works, but I am still in process.

However, I *know* that it does. Sometimes it takes me being down to my last bit of hope to reach out to God and trust his word, but when I finally do, he always comes through. Always. In ways big and small, in whispers and sometimes joyous shouts, he answers.

Let that encourage you today. He is a burst of light in a long darkened room. He always shines through, and we know that first because he did it in days gone by, then we read about it in his word, then he does it again and again in our lives.

Reaching Out...

God, help me to hold on when things seem darkest. Help me not to trust in my own feelings and habits, but to hold fast to your Word. Assure me that when I call on your name, you will answer. Amen.

Reaching In...

1. In what ways are you reminded that God and his Word light your path each day?
2. Do you have a tendency to see the Bible as just a rulebook?
3. Do you find God's Word kind and wooing, or strict and unyielding?

Day 2: God is... Just In Time

Just In Time arrives precisely when he means to
    He enters always at the fullness of time
    Sometimes I feel he is late
    Or he is rudely and prematurely interrupting my plans

But he is Just In Time
He is not bound by time
On the contrary, he commands time and space
    hurling stars backward
Walking through walls
    punishing death's cruel hold on creation

I get tripped up when I attempt to map Just In Time
    onto my grid of grids
Deepening my frustration
It only serves to make his arrival all the more sweet

When my troubles have reached fruition
    and are pregnant with distress
Just In Time shows up, for he brings the answer of answers

But scolding is not in his repertoire
He wounds not, as he knows I already feel
    the sting of my own impatience
And so he turns the page
And propels me to a future of hope
    where he is already waiting for me

Psalm 31:13 (AMP) "My times are in Your hands; deliver me from the hands of my foes and those who pursue me and persecute me."

The Way I See It...

I love the "routineness" of the seasons. Spring always follows winter, Summer Spring, and on and on. Routine gives me comfort and grounds me. That is how God made me.

My Dad never graduated from high school and, although he did well for himself, he never achieved the monetary or educational goals of my brother or even me. Once, years ago, when Dad was visiting my brother, he remarked about how the moon always rises in the east and sets in the west. My brother (and me, had I been there) took issue with this statement. Dad, somewhat wounded I suspect, said, "I might not be smart, but I know where the moon rises and sets." Or, as Forrest Gump would say, "I may not be a smart man, but I know what love is."

I need only remember Dad's statement to feel gently chided, like when God reminds us through the times and seasons that he is always there and will always come back around, just like the moon or the sun. And I need only stop for a moment and trust him to do what he says he will do.

Reaching Out...

God, thank you for coming back around time and again, even when I lose heart and I want to make up my own solution like Abraham and Sarah. And thank you for helping me to see past the end of my nose into an eternity of possibilities that lie waiting, if only I seek you and wait on you. Amen.

Reaching In...

1. In what ways are you reminded that God is always just in time?
2. Have you ever dismissed someone's assertion, only to find out later they were right? Has that happened in your relationship with God?
3. Do you ever feel like God might not show up this time? What are some ways you could make yourself more trusting of him?

3

Day 3: God is... Turner Of Tides

Rapids, pushing me forward, driving me back. An unrestrained tide can be a very scary thing. I am out of control and being taken in a direction I do not wish to go.

Just when I think I am on solid footing, the riptide undercuts my hold on all I trusted in. I am one person, rowing against the furious current, futility apparently my only companion. Panic seems a fitting emotion for this ride.

Worse than anything an amusement park could dream up, this is my life, not only adrift, but listing and failing on rough seas.

At once, Turner of Tides calms the chaos with a wave of his hand. One minute I am cast about, searching for a lighthouse, the next I am in his safe harbor. No matter how many rescues, I am always surprised. And that is part of the joy for Turner of Tides. He changes course often when I least expect, but also in a way that brings him absolute joy.

Like a parent who can't wait to see their child open Christmas presents, Turner of Tides joys to witness our moment of expectant release, when all is made right and the tide is turned once again.

Isaiah 43:2 (NIV) "When you pass through the waters, I will be with you; and when you pass through the rivers, they will not sweep over you."

The Way I See It...

I love the musical "Hello Dolly". In community theater I was cast as Barnaby, the fun-loving assistant store clerk who goes to New York City with his friend Cornelius Hackle. I remember watching the movie version endlessly to try to get my lines just right. One of my favorite songs in the musical is "It Only Takes A Moment" in which Cornelius realizes he is desperately in love with Irene Malloy.

Everyday things in life can turn on a dime like that. Love can happen when we least expect it, as can death, and even paying taxes, although it always comes around the same day every year! But we want the remedy to really hard things in life to be just as instant, and predictable in addition. Hard things like depression, cancer, unemployment, or divorce.

However, I think God tracks with the *un*predictability of the problem. What I mean is, in the same way that our maladies seem to strike at us out the blue, God often uses the same tactic to bring aid. In a moment, he makes all things new. In an instant he can turn the tide. A check in the mail.

An unanticipated gift. A word of encouragement in a difficult time.

A few times I have cried out to him in despair and he has answered me in that moment. But not always. Remember: God is who he is, not who I would have him be. He can repair in a heartbeat, but he is not bound to. But know this: he *will* turn the tide, but you must trust his timing and his tactics.

Reaching Out...

God, help me trust you when I am least likely to. Not just trust you to turn the tide, but to trust you even when you do not. Even though I feel like it, I am not lost and I am not adrift. I hold fast to your unfailing love for me, and the promise that one day all will me made right. Amen.

Reaching In...

1. In what ways are you reminded that God is able to turn the tide in your life?
2. Do you sometimes long for your life, and Gods' part in it, to be more predictable?
3. Is it easier for you to trust God in the middle of trouble, or when you are past it?

4

Day 4: God Is… Treasure Hunter

Treasure Hunter deals not in pick or axe, gold, silver, or gems, but in humanity. Like an ancient Jacob Marley he cries, "Mankind is my business!" Treasure Hunter searches with a relentlessness that knows no equal. Once found, he gives all he has to purchase the treasure.

Scaling great mountains, crossing unbridgeable seas, or tunneling deep into immovable rock, there is no obstacle between he and the treasure that cannot be moved, destroyed, or nullified. Treasure Hunter is up to the job, for he alone knows and appreciates the value instilled in the object of his desire.

Others wonder at his obsession, but Treasure Hunter knows that without his pursuit all will be lost. He defies the naysayers who call up to him, "She is not worth it!" He knows that for a treasure to have any real worth, it must first be wanted. Then it must be found. Then it must be purchased.

Treasure desired. Treasure found
Treasure paid for: IN FULL

Matthew 13:46 (NLT) "When he discovered a pearl of great value, he sold everything he owned and bought it."

The Way I See It...

Jesus spoke of the kingdom of God being like a priceless pearl. That is a great, eternal truth. One day, as I was meditating on this scripture, I made the connection that *we* are also a pearl of great price to him. And God moved heaven and earth, giving his only begotten Son to purchase us. Gives a fresh meaning to *he sold everything he had and bought it* don't you think?

In the novel *True Grit* by Charles Portis, Mattie Ross states resolutely, "Nothing is free except the grace of God." Talk about an author boiling down a great biblical truth. It is free, free, free. Did I mention free? He doesn't want you to add anything to his extravagantly purchased grace. It is bought and paid for. Now he wants to see your face, wide-eyed in wonder, when you, his treasure, exclaim, "You mean it's free?!?"

Reaching Out...

God, I am in wonder that you first loved me. That you first sought me. That you sent your only Son to die for me when

I was utterly lost and undeserving. Help me to connect with that sense of wonder today as I face a hard world that might not know I have value. And help me to see the world as you do: priceless. Amen.

Reaching In...

1. In what ways do you feel like God values you as his great treasure?
2. Have you ever felt worthless? Does knowing that you are God's treasure bring you a sense of priceless worth?
3. Does God's grace seem like a get-out-of-jail-free card? Is that a cheap love or a wonderful prize?

Day 5: God is... Now and Not Yet

Now and Not Yet is a realist.

He is like my doctor who says, "This is going to hurt, but you *will* get better." He leads me through the valley of the shadow of Now, while casting a vision of the sometimes faraway Not Yet.

He gives peace where there should be none. He gives hope where there should be only ashes and dead men's bones. He says, "Wait here" and moves ahead, but he never lets go of my hand.

He is not constrained by time or space. Now and Not Yet throws me a rescue line and hangs onto the rope while he pulls me up. He is well able to be in two (or more) places at once. But he does not let Not Yet dictate Now. The future, at once hopeful and fearsome, does not possess the ability to prophesy the final word. That future day will come, and when it does, Now and Not Yet will be waiting there with open arms, cheering me on.

John 16:33 (NIV) "I have told you these things, so that in me you may have peace. In this world you will have trouble. But take heart! I have overcome the world."

The Way I See It...

Once, when I was quite ill with a stomach bug, my mother took me to the doctor. I was perhaps 13 at the time and had heard doctors and nurses often say pre-shot, "This won't hurt; it will just feel like a mosquito bite."

That wasn't always true, but it didn't hurt much worse. Well, this time, the nurse looked me squarely in the eye and said, "This is going to hurt." No sedative, no local, no encouragement, nothing – just a painful injection of gamma globulin in the buttocks that I will never forget.

God deals with us like that. He does not sugarcoat our circumstances. He says, "In this world you will have trouble," but he also says, "Take heart!" We need a plain dealer in this life. One who can say, simultaneously: *This is going to hurt, but it will get better.* That is God's message of hope and realism, and it gives us courage.

Reaching Out...

God, help me to endure today while anticipating, not fearing, tomorrow. It is so easy to let my thoughts run wild with visions of doom. You have not called me to the easy life, but to a place where I know there is a discipline which *leads to life*. Your yoke is easy and your burden is light. I commit to trusting you, for you have been where I have been, and you will be waiting for me when I rise tomorrow. Amen.

Reaching In...

1. In what ways do you know that God has things under control, both the now and the not yet?
2. When you think of the future, do you feel helpless or hopeful?
3. Do you feel closer to God in suffering, or further away?

Day 6: God Is... Thirst Quencher

In a dry and weary land
    where there is no water, He is Thirst Quencher

Along the never-ending borders of the wasteland
He is a bottomless water pot, full to the brim
Thirst Quencher is everything the world has longed for
All that creation so long groaned for

He gives relief to the parched traveler
    and makes thirst a distant memory
Deserts line up, in succession, to be made green
Full, flourishing, and whole
Dead forests are slaked, then resurrected
Things that were once lifeless and long forgotten
    are now renewed
Alive, and bursting again with the promise

of eternal tomorrows

And just when all containers seem to be nearing empty
Or spent
The fountains of the great deep suddenly burst forth
Proving once again that there is no longing he cannot sate
No thirst he cannot fill to overflowing

John 10:10 (NIV) "The thief comes only to steal and kill and destroy. I have come that they may have life, and have it to the full."

The Way I See It...

The mass of men lead lives of quiet desperation.
– Henry David Thoreau

Something is terribly wrong and needs to be made right. Everyone knows it, but many can't quite put their finger on it. I believe it has everything to do with the Fall of Adam and the desperate straits in which we find ourselves as a result.

Have you ever been really excited about something, only to have that thing completed and realize it never quite fulfilled your expectations? It's really frustrating. That is certainly a common theme in life, but not what God intends. When we look to him for fulfillment we find something altogether uncommon.

I heard the above scripture translated this way once: "I came that they might have life *above the common.*" I must admit I sometimes don't quite feel "above the common". I can barely get "above average" most of the time. But while we must wait to know the exhilaration that awaits us beyond our mortality, we can certainly experience a life that is uncommon.

Today, expect something above the common from God in your life. Today, be "above the common" in someone else's life.

Reaching Out...

God, I often spend days and even weeks in a fog, just going through the motions. I am not bad. I am not good. I am just existing. I long for more. Help me to know that nothing in this life can quite satisfy that longing and not to go looking for it, except in you. And help me to reach out to others who sense that something is desperately wrong and needs to be made right. I know that you are the answer they seek. Amen.

Reaching In...

1. In what ways has God acted as Thirst Quencher in your life?
2. Is life a never-ending series of humdrum, or do you anticipate most days? What comfort do you find in Jesus' words in John 10:10? Is that a comfort you can carry with you today?
3. Think back on a dry time in your life. How did God refresh you during that time?

7

Day 7: God Is... Not Surprised

Not taken aback. Not hoodwinked. Not blindsided.

God is not surprised.

He is not a man that events should overtake him. He sees the end from the beginning and rides upon the waves of time, directing colossal events, raising up an empire here, and pulling down a Nebuchadnezzar there. All in an eternity's work.

He calls from the land of tomorrow, "I am already here, and all is well." He stands astride the constraints of time itself and gives his saints confidence to move without fear. For though they may often be surprised at where they find themselves and in what condition, Not Surprised is supremely untroubled by events.

On the contrary, he is drawing us into the unknown and troubled waters of today. But they are unknown and troubled only to us. For Not Surprised already arrived at today eons past and beckons us – come, and fear not.

Isaiah 46:9-10 (NKJV) "…For I am God, and there is no other; I am God, and there is none like me, declaring the end from the beginning and from ancient times things that are not yet done…"

The Way I See It…

When my father died it is safe to say I was surprised. Add to that dismayed, grief-stricken, confused, heartsick. We once half joked that he would outlive us all. So full of life and happiness, so ready to see what lay ahead.

A massive heart attack changed all that. The unmerciful, bracing jerk of that kind of news is not something one easily forgets. But through those first terrible days I was comforted by the idea that God was not at a loss as to how to respond to me in that dark hour.

It's not like my father's death snuck up on the Almighty. If so, then he is a poor God indeed. And it's not like things got out of hand on planet earth around 4 B.C. and God said, "Well I'd better send in my Son because this whole Old Testament thing is not going to work." No, God knew, from the foundation of the world. And because he sees the end from the beginning, we can be comforted that nothing can overtake us, because God is standing ready. Nothing can approach us that God, in his sovereignty, has not already foreseen; and for which he is not already prepared to give us comfort.

Reaching Out...

God, comfort me with the truth that you see the end from the beginning. I know it in my head, but help me to feel it in my heart. Shepherd me now as I walk through this latest trial and strengthen me with the promise that you have seen tomorrow and you will meet me there with grace enough for the day. Amen.

Reaching In...

1. In what ways has God let you know he is not startled at your circumstances?
2. Are you prone to believing that God is sometimes surprised by events? Remember, it may not be easily recognizable, but you may act is if that were true.
3. Would knowing more fully that God is in control help you to trust him more readily?

8

Day 8: God Is... Home Sweet Home

A refuge. A resting place. A crackling fire burning warm and bright on a cold winter's eve.

Dinner spread wide at a welcoming table. Pipe and slippers waiting beside a favorite chair. Memories of sweet days gone by, evoked by family pictures adorning the wall. "God Bless This House" hung prominently in the entryway.

All powerful symbols, but all temporary and directing us to the true and only meaningful abode. He is the great Home Sweet Home–the place where I can be myself. Don't be fooled: this is not a pig pen; not a place to throw up one's feet on the coffee table. But Home Sweet Home does bid me sit awhile and rest.

Remember the good times and rest up for the day's work ahead. Refuel and renew in this place that is familiar and welcoming and never changes. You *can* go home again, and oh, what a comfort to return again and again to this Home Sweet Home.

Isaiah 66:13 (NIV) "As a mother comforts her child, so will I comfort you."

The Way I See It...

Home is where the heart is. We've all heard that many times but I personally never fully realized the truth of it until after I was married. My mom always said that when I grew up I would find a job, find a wife, settle down, and live in the same place for the rest of my life. I thought the same thing.

I was a somewhat fearful little boy, and we moved around a lot after my parents divorced. It was excruciating. I wanted nothing more than to stay in one place. But after I married I realized that wherever my wife was, that is where I wanted to be. Locale did not matter, only proximity. I could go anywhere and brave anything with the love of this woman, and I did.

In *The Wizard of Oz* Dorothy Gale spends all of her time trying to get back home to Kansas. In the end she realizes that, though there's no place like home, that place lives mostly inside of us. I think that sense of home and hearth, that warm sigh at the end of the day, that sense of wellbeing, is really a reflection of our rest in God. He is our hiding place and our refuge. And we can go anywhere and do anything knowing that he is always there.

Reaching Out...

God, I want to find rest in you. But lately I don't feel restful – I feel fitful. A sense of unrest, like something is not quite right. I ask you to help me find rest in you. And what's more, help me to reach out to others who might need a refuge. I know you are that Home Sweet Home. As that truth begins to resonate within me, give me courage to share it with those around me. Amen.

Reaching In...

1. In what ways has God been a refuge and a "home sweet home" to you?
2. Are your memories of home and family filled with joy? If not, do you find it hard to relate to God as loving Father and refuge?
3. Family has a lot to do with acceptance. Do you feel fully loved and accepted by your family? By God?

Day 9: God Is... Once And For All

He does not require a do-over.

Mulligan is not in his vocabulary. One And Done is his trademark and his seal.

He is "do it right the first time".

Once And For All proclaims that the work is complete, utterly finalized, and that all transgression, past, present and future, has been paid in full. No amount of addition or subtraction can add to or take away from this work, nor can best intentions pad an already sublime plan.

Muttering voices down aged corridors moan that it is not enough. How could it be? More must be done, and done piled upon done, and on and on never to reach an end of things. But Once And For All calls for quiet along the passageways and down the corridors.

And then he whispers: *it is finished*.

1 Peter 3:18 (ESV) "For Christ also suffered once for sins, the righteous for the unrighteousness, to bring us to God."

The Way I See It...

When I was younger I fully believed that Christ's death paid for my sins. But I reasoned that this sacrifice could only cover the sins I had already committed.

As a new Christian, I felt I had an obligation to tow the line and try to be "perfect". If I did do wrong, I needed to quickly ask for forgiveness. The fear of hellfire and damnation haunted me as I worried I might have forgotten to ask for atonement. Slowly I came to the truth that Christ's sacrifice was once for all time. Not only for all who believe, but for all time.

My debt has been paid in full for all time. And far from being a get-out-of-jail-free card that leads me into sin and shame, this grace makes me so thankful that the last thing I want is to harm the One who loves and saved me. "There is therefore now no condemnation for those who are in Christ Jesus." (Romans 8:1) None whatsoever.

Reaching Out...

God, I rejoice that I am truly free! And I praise you that I am not a disappointment in your eyes. On the contrary, you look upon me with joy, as one you have saved. Help me to live everyday in thankfulness for that freedom and to remember that your work on the cross completed my forgiveness. Amen.

Reaching In...

1. In what ways has God shown you his salvation is complete, once and for all?
2. Christ's work on the cross and his resurrection completed salvation. We have only to trust in him and that completed work. Do you find yourself wanting to "do your part" to earn your salvation?
3. Do you know anyone who has ever abused or taken for granted God's grace? If so, what did that look like?

Day 10: God is... My Nightlight

Dark rooms filled with strange noises
   Endless hallways
   Creaking floors that fill me with dread
   The feeling that something is in the dark with me
      and it is not my friend
   A chill of foreboding that nags at me
      like an antagonist who knows all my secrets

Then, in an instant: Light
Not a huge pyre aflame or a vast volcano
      spewing its presence to the world
Not some great gothic candelabra dripping wax
On the contrary, a steady nightlight

Stubborn, yet subtle in its glow; fierce in its tenacity
But always there. Always shining

Always leading and yet holding back
Saying when to move and when to be still
When to walk and when to hold fast

Its light is calm as it waves
    and creates dancing shadows on the wall
Hallways fearful no longer. Noises abated. All is well

Go with courage into that dark night

Psalm 4:8 (NIV) "In peace I will lie down and sleep, for you alone, Lord, make me dwell in safety."

The Way I See It...

There is something warmly comforting about a night light. I wonder why that is? I mean one could just have the whole room lit up and be done with it. But lighting the whole room seems overly indulgent and meaningless. Sometimes you just need a little light to remind you that everything is going to be alright.

In the 1982 movie *ET- the Extraterrestrial*, ET touches Eliot's forehead with a glowing finger and reassures him, "I'll be right here." That's how I see God sometimes. Not this huge presence in our lives (although he is always present), but a warm glow that we carry daily, always reminding us that he is there and he is not silent. The original eternal flame. When I have done all I can, and all I can do is stand, I reach out for that flicker. That glimmer is the hope that I have been waiting for and leads to the way up and out of shadow and gloom.

Reaching Out...

God, sometimes I worry so much it is hard even to sleep. Help me to turn to you when sleep eludes me. Finding peace in the midst of my unrest is your task to fulfill, for I have done all I can do. You, O God, work the night shift, and I trust you with my very life. Amen.

Reaching In...

1. In what warm ways are you reminded daily that God is always there?
2. Are you motivated more by fear or by love?
3. Does our fear show a lack of faith, or is it just part of our humanness?

Day 11: God Is...No Regrets

He would have it no other way.

The perfect plan begets no second thoughts, nor any Plan B. From the beginning, from holy words to tablets of stone, parchment to printing press, there have been no retractions, no corrections, no addendums or second editions.

No Regrets means what he says, and says what he means. He is a Potter, and he sits at his wheel leaving nothing to chance. Base materials, dirt and water, then the breath of life. Then Adam begets a world, first full of hope, then regret, then dismay, and finally panic. But No Regrets stays at his wheel and works, for he knows how the story ends and what is its purpose: The restoration of all things!

And so he smiles and he works, he laughs and he heals, with never so much as a "what if" or "perhaps I shouldn't have".

No Regrets knows what he is up to, and it is very good.

Psalm 32:1 (NIV) "Blessed is the one whose transgressions are forgiven, whose sins are covered."

The Way I See It...

When I was about 4 years old my parents noticed a change in my behavior. It was subtle at first, but became more pronounced when I started to act lethargic and wanted to be carried all the time.

Things came to a head one chilly Halloween. Everything was otherwise normal: a crisp autumn evening with an overcast Charlie Browny sky, the moon playfully following us as we walked. But something was amiss: on this, the night of all nights for walking, I refused to budge as we trick-r-treated around our little neighborhood. My dad, frustrated at not knowing what to do and tired of carrying me, spanked me. Not too much later it was discovered that my lethargy was caused by a red blood cell disorder that almost mad and end of me.

A few months before Dad passed away I asked him about that night. I only knew the story because he had told me in the first place. He still had a great deal of shame and regret over how he acted, even though he could not have known. It had been decades but the look on his face made it seem like it had just happened.

It was a vivid picture to me of how our actions, even innocent ones, can follow and mock us. Regret is a brutal overlord, and we mustn't let it master us. I made sure Dad knew that he was not to blame. You need to know that God has forgiven you, as well. Don't let regret hold you back from the life he has for you.

Reaching Out...

God, I know we all serve someone or something, even if it is ourselves. I don't want to serve my regrets by attending to them day after day. Please help me to let go of them as they are cast into your sea of forgetfulness. I want to be freely loved and to freely love. As I lay aside these weights, I will turn what was useless effort into love focused outward to you and a hurting world. Amen.

Reaching In...

1. In what ways are you reminded that God is very pleased with you?
2. What is your deepest regret? Are you in danger of letting it master you?
3. We cannot change the past, but God can change our perception of it through forgiveness. Can you remember a regret or past hurt that God has redeemed?

Day 12: God is... Singer Over Me

The orchestra tunes as the virtuoso waits in the wings.

All is set. The stage is lit.

It is the concert of the ages and, as angels dance, the Lord of Hosts steps onto the stage and begins to sing in exultant voice that defies description. The hall is vast in its expanse, and made even more so by the fact that there is an audience of only one: me.

All of this pomp and rejoicing over something as pitiful and scorn-worthy as me.

And yet, the music does not cease. On the contrary, it continues to rise, the Artist pulling each phrase forward with a delicate balance of skill and creativity. The orchestra ebbs and flows as it follows his every note, with a triumphant cascade that fades into a lovesong-lullaby as he sings me softly to sleep.

Supremely comforted, I am secure in the knowledge that he is my God and I am his child.

Sweet peace.

Zephaniah 3:17 (NIV) "He will take great delight in you; in his love he will no longer rebuke you, but will rejoice over you with singing."

The Way I See It...

Alas for those that never sing, But die with all their music in them.
– Oliver Wendell Holmes

I wouldn't know what that is like, because I can't stop singing! Since my earliest memories I wanted to be a musician generally and a singer specifically. My mother laughs about how I could sing every commercial on TV, with little knowledge about what I was singing.

There is something about singing that simultaneously releases and expresses an otherwise inexpressible joy or deep sorrow, and that somewhere in the universe someone is listening and understanding, even when I am completely alone. I used to think that God sang dirges or sad country songs over me, because I was such a disappointment. But over time I came to the realization that God is thrilled with me. Shocking, you say? Perhaps.

What I mean is, I used to think that my behavior was generally frowned upon by God, unless I did something really noticeable, like leading a Sunday school class or donating blood. And even then, it was expected. But slowly, through a lot of prayer and living, listening to good, godly people, understanding scripture, and raising my kids, I realized that God's love for me is not based on my performance.

Because of his grace I am inclined to "do good", but whether or not I do it, he still loves me. And not a "He-has-to-because-He-is-God" love. It is a love for the ages. It knows no limits and holds nothing back. I had such a smallish conception of God's love for me. I'm glad that's over with.

Reaching Out...

God, I know I am your child, but often I feel like I never do enough to please you. Remind me today that your love for me is strong and that my hope in you is secure. When I close my eyes I see you singing over me. Not for anything in particular, but just because. Amen.

Reaching In...

1. In what ways are you reminded that God joys over you with singing?
2. Is your life a never-ending effort to please? Does that affect your relationship with God?
3. What would you tell someone who feels unacceptable to God?

Day 13: God Is... Dream Granter

Not daydreamer. Not Lollygagger. Not Lay-about.

Dream Granter tirelessly works the night shift. When all have bidden the day a long goodbye, along with its spent promise, what might've been, and lost hope, he sets about making things right.

Check that: Dream Granter sets about making things better. Exceedingly, abundantly better. Better than new car better. We ask for a stone, and He gives us bread. We settle for water, and he gives us wine overflowing. Dream Granter knows what makes the world tick. A dream is that which is not expected. It is that which could not be foreseen. By its very nature, a dream can't rightly be put into proper words even to ask it.

And so, Dream Granter takes our request filled with hope, mixes it with the infinite "what could be" and imminent potential, and turns our world upside down with a dream for the ages. One that we, upon waking, could not imagine nor we will we soon forget.

Ephesians 3:20 (TLB) "Now glory be to God, who by his mighty power at work within us is able to do far more than we would ever dare to ask or even dream of – infinitely beyond our highest prayers, desires, thoughts, or hopes."

The Way I See It…

Sometimes the dream we are granted is the one we never asked for, but the one we really wanted and needed all the time. I never wanted to be a worship leader. In fact, it didn't even make the Top Ten list of musical careers I had in mind. I had no desire to do the same thing week to week, waving my arms around in front of a bunch of people. But Dream Granter knew better.

Through a series of circumstances I found myself leading worship at a little church in Marshall, Texas in 1995. I had no other prospects, and they offered health insurance, so I had nothing to lose and much to gain. After a few years of leading worship I had an epiphany: this is what I am supposed to do. Oh man…this is what I am supposed to do! Talk about "far more than we would ever dare to ask or even dream of". This was it, brother. I often joke to people that if I had known God's plan for my life from the start I would have loused it up.

We have a cruel success rubric by which we measure our lives and our worth. But think *Mr. Holland's Opus*, in which a music teacher realizes that the thing he has shunned for most of his life is actually the thing that gives his life meaning and purpose.

Often we find that God is up to something of which we are not even aware and will surprise us supremely. Open your eyes to the possibility that while you have been planning and dreaming, God has been working the night shift and bringing about something that is infinitely beyond your highest prayers, desires, thoughts, or hopes.

Reaching Out...

God, I still have big dreams! Some of them I have given up on, and I wonder if my best years are past. But I know you have big dreams for me, too. Whisper deep into my soul today that you are still in the business of fulfilling destiny. I know my hopes and dreams are precious to you, and I trust you with them. Amen.

Reaching In...

1. In what ways are you reminded that God has great plans for you?
2. Have you ever avoided something, only to find out later it is exactly what you needed?
3. What did you want to be when you were young? Did that come to fruition?

14

Day 14: God Is... Storm Calmer

The lightning cracks
   The gale howls and spits and moans
   The earth shudders and rumbles, first low and deep
   Then loud and crashing

And Storm Calmer
     like some great adventuring swashbuckler
Climbs the mast of an ancient vessel
     dagger in teeth and sword in hand
With a singular purpose: to tame the tempest
He has power enough in reserve to still all
But sometimes taming is all that is needed

Storm Calmer walks upon the very waves he stills
A smooth glass pane beneath his nimble feet
The water laps at his soles, like a subdued and scolded beast

But this great power is not braggadocio
It has a meaning and a purpose: to calm the soul of his child

The heavens and all the angels of creation shout his praise
But this child is his highest concern
Cloud and rain must be redirected
    wind and wave must be chided

Finally, in the distance, only a blowing breeze
    is faintly heard skipping across still waters
For now, all is well, safe, and at rest

Mark 4:39 (NASB) "And he got up and rebuked the wind and said to the sea, 'Hush, be still.' And the wind died down and it became perfectly calm."

The Way I See It...

Storm chasing is on my bucket list, so you can imagine why I love the movie *Twister*. It has everything: action, adventure, suspense, a love story, and bad weather. It was a lot scarier the first time I watched it, as I wasn't quite sure how it would all end. I am fascinated at how the tornado is raging at one moment, and then disappears with just a whiff of falling debris.

  Life storms are sometimes like that. We are just starting to sweat when we see it is all over. What a relief. But other storms are not so easily weathered. In fact, they are breathtakingly brutal: broken relationships, sickness, pain, death. Each leaves its own particular brand of scars and wreckage. It is in the midst of these times, when life is out of control, that God whispers as only he can, and says, "I am here and I love you." There is a scene in *Forrest Gump* where Lieutenant Dan is hanging from the shrimp boat's mast in a fierce storm, shaking his fist at God out of anger and exasperation. Then, having braved the storm and gotten the answer he sought, he is finally at peace.

It's ok to question God. David did. We won't ever have all the answers to all the questions we ask. But be honest. He can take it. He loves you that much. And he will calm the storm.

Reaching Out...

God, help me to be brave enough when the storms come to be open with you. I know that not all of my storms will be stilled outside, but I ask you to settle the waves inside. If I can have your peace that passes understanding I know I can face anything. My hope is in you. Amen.

Reaching In...

1. In what ways are you reminded that God is your Storm Calmer?
2. What storm are you facing right now? Can you trust God even though you don't know the outcome?
3. If God calmed all of your life storms, would you lean on him more or less? Do you think perhaps these storms

have a deeper life-changing purpose that we cannot see?

15

Day 15: God Is... Gift Giver

Gift Giver is lavish in his extravagance. He courses the globe in search of the finest tokens, in hopes that his beloved will know the depths of his love.

Having already laid down his life, all other gifts pale in comparison, and yet still he lavishes. He pours out.

He displays his winsomeness again and again, not because he needs to, but because he need not. He spares no expense to give the finest things, then spies a tiny trinket that costs only a pittance. He knows, however, that this small thing will mean a great deal to his beloved, though it costs little and takes hardly an effort. Such a small thing, but imbued with such meaning. Like a cup of water given to one dying in the desert. Such a small thing, but such a gift!

James 1:17 (NIV) "Every good and perfect gift is from

above, coming down from the Father of the heavenly lights, who does not change like shifting shadows."

The Way I See It...

Sometimes it's the little things. I wrote most of this devotional at a home on Toledo Bend Lake in East Texas. The last time I was there I was with my dad. Being there again brought back so many memories and emotions.

Soon after my arrival I was walking around, remembering the places we spoke: a porch over here, under a shade tree over there. Little chats and small moments, suddenly painfully remembered as larger than life. Instantly I blurted out, "God, it would really mean a lot to me if you could give me a dream of my dad tonight." Request granted.

That night I had the most wonderful dream about my dad, my brother, and me. When I awoke I heard God speak quietly to my soul, "I am here and I love you."

God delights in giving gifts, great and small, to his children. He is in the gift-giving business. Grace is his greatest gift, but he gives daily in small ways that sometimes go unnoticed. Look around you today and notice the good things he is sending your way. Tune your senses to the small ways he shows his big love. If you set your mind to it, I'll bet you can think of a dozen off the top of your head. Use today to think on those things and give him thanks.

Reaching Out...

God, forgive me for overlooking all of the little ways you show me your love and care. Help me to remember that you don't require my gratitude, but you love it when I offer it freely. I recognize your good, gift-giving character today, and it fills me with gladness. Amen.

Reaching In...

1. In what ways are you reminded that God delights in being the Gift Giver?
2. What is the best material gift you have ever received? What was so great about it?
3. Name some seemingly "mundane" gifts for which you can be thankful every day.

Day 16: God Is... Good All the Time

God is righteous, but don't forget that God is love.
God is supreme, but don't forget that God is merciful.
God is great, but don't forget that God is Good.
He both *is* good and *does* good.
The evil one tears at the reputation of the Good One. "Skin for skin!" he hisses, as he lies about who this Good One is. That infernal serpent knows that if he can convince us God is no longer good, then God is no longer great. And so, lie upon lie he builds an edifice that has as its foundation the idea that God is not really good, but selfish and a withholder of good things.
But it only takes the breath of God to vanquish this tower of treachery. His resume is ancient. His very nature is to do good all the time, and he will not stand for the besmirching of his reputation. So the evil foundation is cracked at the sound of his voice, and the word goes forth that God is supreme.

God is righteous.
God is Great.
And God is Good. All the time.

Nahum 1:7 (NASB) "The Lord is good, a Stronghold in the day of trouble, and he knows those who take refuge in him."

The Way I See It...

One of the great lies of the devil is to convince us that God is withholding some good thing from us. This insidious idea can give us just the inspiration we need to doubt his essential goodness and seek satisfaction somewhere else. But God's word shows us again and again we can trust that He will be good to us.

In the garden Satan told Eve that God was withholding good by restricting the tree. Such a lie! God, by his edict, was being good in trying to protect them. C.S. Lewis said it like this: *"There is but one good, that is God."*

One thing I have learned in life is this: you can be completely convinced of something… and be completely wrong. At one time I was convinced that God was a cosmic killjoy and just wanted to spoil my fun. I know now that God's delight is not in pointing out my broken road, but in setting me on the straight path. In the words of Tolkien's Gandalf, *"I'm not trying to rob you, Bilbo Baggins! I'm trying to help you."*

Our good God is not trying to withhold good things from us, he is trying to help us. We often do not see it that way, because we still see through human eyes that have been dimmed by sin. But we can trust that he is good. *You* can trust that he is good. Today you can trust him with your very life.

Reaching Out...

God, I want to trust you today. But sometimes I feel selfish and afraid. This makes me feel like you are withholding good things from me even though in my heart I know it's not true. Remind me of your goodness today and help me to be a reflection of that goodness to others in everything I do and say. Amen.

Reaching In...

1. In what ways are you reminded that God is good all the time?
2. Does thinking God is withholding some good thing make it easier to slip into sin?
3. Have you ever come to the realization that you were completely wrong about something or someone in which you had trusted?

17

Day 17: God Is… Burden Lifter

A living weight mocks with an uncomfortable familiarity, like a once old and dear friendship gone sour and poisonous. It climbs upon the shoulders, breathing down my neck as if to taunt my already harried soul.

As the path grows long, the burden grows greater, trouble upon trouble piling up, until at last it seems the great heap must topple. Alas, instead of falling away, it only climbs down deeper inside me, steadying the balance, but crushing my very existence.

Then subtly… and suddenly… Burden Lifter reaches out to touch my uneasy and aching back, and steady my trembling knees. Hopeful, I feel he is going to tear away my pack in an instant. But he pauses. And as he pauses he leans in. Then he speaks softly and sweetly into my waiting ear comforts so dear, assurances so blessed, and promises so true.

I arrived at his door for the burden lifting that I had in

mind… but he had something far better in store: a comfort that words could scarce describe, nor heart contain. Wonderful words that do more than lift a burden: they carry me through and keep me going.

Burden Lifter knows I must grow, and so he sends me down the rough, narrow way, but not without provision. Once again, my burden is lightened as I walk on down the trail that leads to Life.

Galatians 5:1 (NLT) "It is for freedom that Christ has set us free. Stand firm, then, and do not let yourselves be burdened again by a yoke of slavery."

The Way I See It…

In the book *Pilgrim's Progress* by John Bunyan, the main character, named Christian, is on a journey in which he carries a heavy, burdensome pack on his back. At a defining point he arrives at the cross and the burden spontaneously falls from its perch.

When I read that book in high school the import of that moment was lost on me. I knew Christ had saved me, but I thought, "I must do my part. I must keep up my end of the bargain." Little did I realize that God's love is so radical, so controversial, so scandalous, that it required that I simply believe. There was nothing to do on my part, as far as gaining salvation. And that, to quote Robert Frost, "has made all the difference".

What a relief knowing that God loves me no matter what,

and that I am accepted, no matter what. Whenever you think you might need to do something in order to gain God's love or his favor, just remind yourself: I am free. It's true – you are free, indeed.

Reaching Out...

God, as soon as I release one burden, another seems to take its place. Help me to trust you, not just as the one who looses my burdens, but as the one who gives me strength to walk through the trials. I don't want to be a slave to anyone or anything except you. Amen.

Reaching In...

1. In what ways are you reminded that God is a burden lifter?
2. Was there a time when you were enslaved to something? Did you find it easier at times to live in that enslavement rather than risk freedom?
3. Do you find yourself wanting to do things to gain God's favor?

Day 18: God Is... Closer than a Brother

A kinship. A bond
   Ties that bind and cords that cannot be broken
   Relationship that began in a garden, bursting in bloom
   And still bringing life to dark things in dark places
      where mortal hearts go to die
   Closer than a Brother sticks to his guns
   He is brother and keeper, redeemer and restorer

I am in prison and he visits me
I am naked and he clothes me
     I am sick and he comes to my aid
That's what family is for. That's what brothers do
He knows where I have been, for he has been there, too
And lived to tell about it

Even more, he conquered what I am just now facing
He cries, he weeps, he bleeds with me
He offers hope where none seems possible or even plausible
And he stands by my side
    not over me, or behind, or too far ahead
Shoulder to shoulder, staring down life together

And if there is anything on the trail ahead
    he promises to scold it -
        whether lightless room or dragon's fire
Or if necessary, to dispatch it with extreme prejudice

The Darkness knows that Closer than a Brother
    is my boon companion
So he comes around only infrequently
And when he does show up he fights dirty
    but my champion knows all his wiles

And so, Closer than a Brother keeps me near
    and walks beside me
Shoulder to shoulder, arm in arm
    beating back the darkness
That's what family is for. That's what brothers do

Proverbs 18:24 (ESV) "A man of many companions may come to ruin, but there is a friend who sticks closer than a brother."

The Way I See It...

When we were boys my older brother and I were together all the time. He was my hero and fearless. I, on the other hand, felt fearful a lot of the time, and sometimes I got picked on.

One older boy named John was particularly ruthless. He teased and taunted me on the school bus and generally made my life miserable. I was too little to do anything about it, but my brother was the same age as John. One day my brother had enough. He told John to meet him on the trail behind our home (neutral territory). A big group of kids, including me, gathered to see what would happen.

My brother had the distinct advantage of having something to fight for. His passion was kindled and I doubt he remembered much after the first punch. John was a bully, and he got what most bullies get when challenged: he was vanquished in short order. Oh heck, my brother stomped a mudhole in him and walked it dry.

Imagine how God feels about you compared to your closest friend or family member. He is closer. He will go to the mat for you. There is no difficulty he has not endured for you. He wept in agony in the garden for you; he bled on Calvary for you. That's not a guilt trip. It's a truth that can give you comfort when all have run out on you. When all else has failed there is a friend who sticks closer than a brother.

Reaching Out...

God, help me to remember that you love me like no other.

I will never be alone because you will always be by my side. Give me the strength to be a friend, brother, or sister to someone in need today. Amen.

Reaching In...

1. In what ways are you reminded that God is like one who sticks closer than a brother?
2. Do you have memories of being bullied? How was it resolved? Were you ever the bully?
3. Jesus told his disciples in John 15 (NIV), *"I no longer call you servants, because a servant does not know his master's business. Instead, I have called you friends, for everything that I learned from my Father I have made known to you."* Does the idea of being God's friend feel comforting or unseemly?

Day 19: God Is... New Every Morning

Darkness, thick and black, covers all
   A blanket of heaviness, overlain with a confusing fog
   Waiting seems like a thousand deaths
   Hope is teetering, wavering, waning, almost spent
   Then...suddenly...light breaks through the veil of sorrow

   Tears give way to shouts of joy
   New Every Morning has arrived once again
      with bright, fresh hope
   He was here yesterday, and the day before
      and the day before
   But the newness never grows old
   His mercies are New Every Morning!

For a moment I recall that this has happened so often before, but then I realize: never like this. In fact, he was New

Every Morning just last week, and it seemed like the first time. Like a bridegroom coming to meet the bride for the first time.

He never grows old. His message of hope never ceases, never sours or fades. Just when I think that I have reached the end of all his surprises, he reaches down deep from his wellspring and pours forth anew an encouragement, a song, a hope.

Whatever it happens to be that morning, it is just what I need. Just in time, but never the same.

New… every morning.

Lamentations 3:22-23 (ESV) "The steadfast love of the Lord never ceases; his mercies never come to an end; they are new every morning; great is your faithfulness."

The Way I See It…

Clearly, God's mercies are new every morning, but in a way so is he.

My mother once told me, "You have to *make* yourself happy." I used to be a slave to my emotions. If I woke up in a bad mood I would just resign myself to the idea that I was going to be grumpy that day. Now, my mom's words are not the end of the subject, but only the beginning. A jumping-off point, if you will. I have to at least decide that I have the choice to be happy. But sometimes it is *really* hard to be content when you are going through a crisis. But God is faithful and he can give you a joy in the midst of suffering that feels new every day.

I don't know how it works exactly, but I do know that if I sit and suffer nothing will change. But if I look for God to show up, he often does in unexpected ways, newly every day. Sometimes you may feel like Bill Murray in *Groundhog Day*, just going through the motions. But in an instant you could wake up to a whole new world, a whole new understanding of God. Reach out to him and expect that he will work in your life. He will do it. His mercies are new every morning.

Reaching Out...

God, sometimes it feels as if the darkness is thick, and I am going through the motions trying to keep my head above water. I ask you to lift up my countenance and restore joy to my heart. Be new to me today in a way I have never experienced or expected before. Amen.

Reaching In...

1. In what ways are you reminded that God's mercies are new every morning?
2. Have you ever had to *decide* to be happy despite your circumstances?
3. Is it possible to be unhappy yet content? Think of an example.

Day 20: God Is… Pursuer

Across vast oceans of time
   Like the Prodigal's father running to meet him
   Pursuer bridges the gulf in an instant
   Girding his regal robes, he sprints toward the prize
   Valleys are built up, mountains humbled
      and made a smooth plain
   So that Pursuer may cross unhindered

He rejoices to run his course
      as the rising sun exults in the break of day
For all of humanity is his prize
A wreathed olive crown placed upon his brow
      at the moment of victory
From book to book, Genesis to Revelation
His pace is seen across the pages
Ever quickening his step until finally his work is done

All creation rests, race won
    swords into plowshares, spears into pruning hooks
Every wrong made right
He cannot be stopped, he will not be held back
He strains forward
    reaching toward the final goal of restoration
The crowd roars, then sighs with relief
The great Pursuer has run his race and won
    beat the clock and vanquished every foe

Romans 5:8 (NIV) "But God demonstrates his own love for us in this: While we were still sinners, Christ died for us."

The Way I See It...

When I read the above verse I revel in the fact that all of it was planned before the foundation of the world. Amazing to think about: that he would go to such lengths to redeem us who were still dead in our sins. Make no mistake: He does not wait for you to become "acceptable". There is no human behavior that can make you acceptable. God seeks us and simply asks that we believe his word.

I wrote a song called *Father To the Orphan*, and one of the verses says:

> *"You're my brother, you're my keeper*
> *when I'm lost you are a seeker*
> *When I fall you pick me up with your big, strong hands*

> *You're a Father to this orphan, lost and alone, out in the cold*
> *Then you brought me home…"*

Those metaphors remind us how God sought and pursued us even before we were even aware of him or his plan. As St. Augustine said, "By loving us, God makes us loveable." Even before I knew I needed help, he was pursuing me. Even after I have come to believe in him, he continues to pursue, to woo, and to welcome.

Does it heighten your sense of worth to know that he would go to such great lengths to win you to himself? It should!

Reaching Out…

God, thank you for reminding me that you loved me before I even thought about being "good". You loved me in my sin, and you love me now. Give me that compassion for others and help me to pursue them with your message of hope and love. Amen.

Reaching In…

1. In what ways are you reminded that God continues to pursue you?
2. Does the idea that God sought and seeks you fill you with appreciation?
3. Have you ever relentlessly pursued something until you found it? How did it make you feel?

Day 21: God Is... Extravagant

He spares no expense
    He is a giver from the start
        before the foundation of the world
    He loves so much that he gives until it hurts
    And gives and gives and gives

    Wooing us like a lover who maintains the greatest of hope
    That his love will not remain unrequited
    He is diamonds and rubies, sapphires and emeralds
    Gold, silver, and pearls without end
    And yet that does not begin to describe
    He is a red rose; blood red
    Gushing forth forgiveness and this extravagant love

    In great wave upon wave of tender devotion
        that calls out across the ages

"I love you! I am waiting for you, and my patience is long
My mercies deep, and the rivers of my peace are wide"
The banks of that river are widest at the moments
    of our deepest sorrows and tragedies
Filling up and overwhelming the tumult of our lives
With a comfort bought with a steep price

His vast storehouse is inexhaustible
His compassion an immense, heaving cistern
    Filled to the top
        ever increasing, never ceasing
And across the ages
    Extravagant sends the message of the cross:
All is forgiven
You have naught to do, only believe
Love Has Conquered All!

John 3:16 (NASB) "For God so loved the world that he gave his only begotten Son, that whoever believes in him shall not perish, but have everlasting life."

The Way I See It...

In the play *Death of a Salesman* by Arthur Miller, Willy Loman has a great, driving need: to be well-liked. He believes it the most important quality in achieving success. I often suffer from the same affliction. I just want everyone to like me, especially God. I mean, that would be a considerable feat in itself, wouldn't it? Just to be "liked" by God?

I get too used to the idea of God's love sometimes and I forget how much he loves me and what it cost him: his only begotten son, Jesus. I remind myself of that, not as an emotional bludgeon, but as a reminder that God doesn't just like me, he loves me! But, and this is really great, too: he likes me! To paraphrase Sally Field in her iconic 1985 Oscar acceptance speech, "He really likes us!!"

It's hard to doubt his love for us when the evidence for it is piled up. The Bible is not a book about various people and their dealings with God. Well, it is that, but it is so much more. It is God's love story to us. His love whispers through each page. From Adam's fall to Revelation's closing encouragement, the redemption story of God's love is laid bare for all to see. Open your eyes, attend your ears. Hear him sing his extravagant love song to you this day.

Reaching Out...

God, you love me so much, and that love is so divinely extravagant. Thank you for doing more than just enough. You surprise me every day with the immensity of your love. Help me to love others with that same extravagance. Amen.

Reaching In...

1. In what ways are you reminded that God lavishes his love on you?
2. Are there times when you have withheld good things from someone who hurt you?

3. When you hear the word "extravagant" does it conjure up negative feelings or positive?

Day 22: God Is... Liberator

I am a sparrow, trapped
   From the fowler's snare there seems no escape
      no way out, no way through
I'll not fly away any time soon
   for shackled I appear to timeless be
Disturbingly comfortable, I linger in my little cage

But a nudging sense of hope, from out of nowhere, appears
And dread begins to retreat from its perch within my soul
From behind the curtain of eternity
   Liberator steps into my prison and smiles
Not the glib smile of uncaring
   or unfeeling or a cavalier pose
But one of assurance, of a secret begging to be told

The secret he bears is this:

From ages past he has been
    and will always be Liberator
He comes to deliver me
From evil. From destruction. From oppression
    From mere inconsequence
In short, he comes to liberate me out of darkness
    and deliver into glorious light

As he reaches in, I lash out
My humanness fears that his touch means theft
But his arms extend with love and healing, and for freedom
And freedom I shall have
Freedom in fact. Freedom Indeed

1 Peter 2:9 (NIV) "But you are a chosen people, a royal priesthood, a holy nation, God's special possession, that you may declare the praises of him who called you out of darkness into his wonderful light."

The Way I See It...

The 2010 movie *True Grit* begins with a line from Proverbs 28... *"The wicked flee where none pursue."* It provokes thoughts of a guilty conscience, of never being able to find rest. I have felt like that a few times. But whether or not one has committed a great offense or a small one, we all have those tinges of guilt. Even when we have done nothing "wrong" sometimes we can feel guilty anyway.

    I chalk it up to being a child of Adam. After all, we are

born in sin no matter how good or bad we are or act, and we are without hope on our own. But that sobering fact sends me hurtling toward someone, something, some outside force that can offer hope of rescue from such hopelessness. That someone is Jesus. His death and resurrection are the one sure cure to life's chaos and meaninglessness.

This is true liberation: Grace does not simply say you who are guilty may go free. Grace says you are not guilty.

Reaching Out...

God, though I am utterly guilty, you count me not guilty because Jesus took my place. Remind me that I am your precious possession, bought with an awful price. I am thankful to you today and every day for this great gift. Amen.

Reaching In...

1. In what ways are you reminded that God is your liberator?
2. Are there times when you have been "disturbingly comfortable" in your life? What brought you out of it?
3. How does freedom in Christ not lead to license?

Day 23: God is... Good News

I used to believe
    I used to believe that God was disappointed
    I used to believe he was arbitrary and capricious
    A cosmic killjoy
    I used to believe he accepted me if I did the right things

If I said the right words
If I behaved accordingly
If I worked harder…prayed longer…
I used to believe God was Bad News all around
But he was the only game in town, so believe I did

Then God uttered Good News into my waiting ear
This Good News filled my longing heart
His timely word spoke of complete acceptance
Of love amazing, grace divine

Like a long awaited message from a dear friend
    his words refreshed

I found that God truly is good, all the time
I found acceptance
I found completion
I found it was not about my doing
    but about his having DONE
Once and for all

I found the one missing part that has settled the matter
And made all the difference

Proverbs 25:25 (NASB) "Like cold water to a weary soul, so is good news from a distant land."

The Way I See It...

I have developed this habit of thinking the worst in any given situation, just in case things get really bad. Things rarely end as badly as I fear, and so I am rarely taken by surprise at life's little spitballs. However, I made the mistake early on of thinking that way about God as well. I had the Almighty figured for a tyrant; a schoolmaster who towered over me with his ruler, waiting for me to make the slightest mistake so he could smack the back of my hand.

  I don't know what I was thinking, because I was good at making BIG mistakes! But once real life got ahold of me I realized that there had to be something more to being a

Christian than doing all the "right" things. That is when I came to grips with true grace, and the fact that God simply bids me to come, to drink, to believe that he loves me incomparably. I'll tell you right now, I felt like Solomon who said, *"Good news from a distant land is like cold water for a weary person."*

The moment you think God might be disappointed in you, think again. He is desperately in love with you. Read his love story, the Bible, and see just how far he went to prove that love to you. That is Good News indeed.

Reaching Out...

Lord, sometimes I feel like I am on autopilot. I wake up, I go through my daily routine, I come home, I go to sleep. I miss the joy and freshness that I once hailed as Good News. Revive in me again the joy of that priceless salvation. Restore the freshness of our relationship. I know you will do as you have promised. Help me to rest in that promise. Amen.

Reaching In...

1. In what ways are you reminded that God's message is one of Good News?
2. Are there things you used to believe about God that you have discarded?
3. In what ways has God surprised you with his goodness?

Day 24: God Is... Unseen

Blackness enfolds and presses in like a blanket
    First tightly, then lovingly
    The darkness mystifies and beckons
    Comforts and soothes
    Terror should be here somewhere
        but is conspicuously absent

To let go is to begin to love
To trust even the unseen
Letting go feels like defeat, then unknowing
    and finally relief

Relief in knowing that in his mysterious way
    he performs wonders untold
"Deep in unfathomable mines of never failing skill
He treasures up His bright designs

    and works His sovereign will"
He is Unseen, but not Unknown or Unfelt

He comforts the afflicted
Shelters the hurting
Guides the weary
Rescues the wayward from the pit

And finally, in the last moments of death
    a familiar hand reaches from the darkness
"Come up here
    I will show you great and incomprehensible things
        you know not"

Psalm 97:1-2 (KJV) "The Lord reigneth; let the earth rejoice; let the multitude of isles be glad thereof. Clouds and darkness are round about him: righteousness and judgment are the habitation of his throne."

The Way I See It...

I have a very dear friend who lost his young daughter to cancer. In my shared grief over his loss and not knowing what I could do, I penned this sober reflection:

"I am a man of little courage. My friend stands at the rim of the abyss and steels himself as he peers over the edge. I can but gaze upon the bewildering scene, pray, and shudder. Nevertheless, blessed be the name of The Lord."

My friend knows something about peering into deep

darkness. He has gazed into what would seem unfathomable, and yet he did not recoil. Somewhere inside that chasm God reached out to he and his family and gave them grace to endure. I only pray that I might experience that same grace when I face such a trial.

My point is that in all of our knowing we still serve a God who is unseen. We see his works, but our physical eyes do not see him. But somehow, his "unseen-ness" is strangely comforting. I peer into the deep, black night sky and I know he is there. I reach out into the chaos and find a God waiting to comfort me always. My friend dared to stare into the abyss and knew that God would meet him with sufficient comfort. Overwhelming comfort, in fact.

We don't have to know and see everything. We just have to know that "God's got this". Don't be afraid of the dark. God is right there with you. He who dwells in deep darkness will comfort you just like he comforts my friend.

Reaching Out...

God, I do not need to know everything. I do not need to see you to know that you love me and want the best for me. Help me to remember you every day even though I don't see you with my eyes or hear you with my ears. Guide me in paths of righteousness for your name's sake. Amen.

Reaching In...

1. In what ways are you reminded that God, though

unseen, is more present than anything you could ever touch, see, or feel?
2. What is the worst thing you have faced so far in life? How did God meet you there and bring you through it?
3. Were you afraid of the dark as a child? Are you still? What about the darkness can be comforting and reassuring?

Day 25: God Is... In Control

A crisp, brown leaf wafts in the autumn wind
   A flower grows, withers, and dies
   Sparrow flies, sparrow falls
   None knows where or how they will end

Heads bear down and push through bitter cold
   Hoping for a reprieve from the icy tingle of life's chill grip
   All seems slightly off, like a fiddle string
      stretched a bit too tightly
   Like the Almighty has taken holiday

Providence waxes cruel, distant, and unnerving
   The Lord giveth and the Lord taketh away
   Future unknown is rushing headlong into future bleak
   Little is making sense, and much seems nonsense

But trust calls out to let go and walk on into the unknown
To recognize the One who can make sense of nonsense
The One who hovered over the face of the deep
Said, "Let there be light" and "Peace, be still"

The One who walked upon the cresting waves
It is He who created the elements
    who flung the stars into their places
And set their courses
He gently calls out to the troubled soul…
"I am still in control, I am here, trust me"

Psalm 103:19 (NASB) "The Lord has established his throne in the heavens, and his sovereignty rules over all."

The Way I See It…

Charles Spurgeon said, "*Visit many good books, but live in the Bible*". The Bible is the most important book I have ever read. But there is another book that is second on my list of life-changing works. It is called *Embracing the Love of God* by James Bryan Smith. I recommend it highly. Referencing G.K. Chesterton, he writes:

"*Nature is not a system of necessity. Yes, the sun will probably come up tomorrow, but it need not. Perhaps each day God says to the sun, 'Arise! Go forth!' …there are no 'laws' of nature. God can do whatever he wishes. It is not a necessity, for though we can count on it practically, we have no right to say that it must always happen."*

I love the idea that God would take that amount of care in his creation. *Arise! Go forth!* I love even more that he is a loving God of infinite detail, not an unfeeling, random force of nature. He cares for his creation, in which you and I play a vital role. Nothing is going to happen that he does not already know about.

A friend once reminded me God is never surprised. That sounds so simple, but when I would find myself in a bad situation I would often cry out to God as if I were informing him of a new bit of news about which he hadn't a clue had I not let him in on the situation. But God is already standing in my tomorrow, knowing what I will face when I get there. Perhaps you, like me, already know this. It's nice to be reminded, though, don't you agree?

Reaching Out...

God, I long to be in control of every area of my life. In fact, to be out of control equals panic for my insides. Help me to trust you enough to let you have daily control of my life. And help me try not to control others as well! Amen.

Reaching In...

1. In what ways are you reminded that God is in control?

2. Do you ever feel like you are "informing" God of some bit of bad news?
3. Have you ever felt like your suffering was out of control, i.e. that even God might not be in control?

Day 26: God Is... Nevertheless

nev·er·the·less
   nevərTHə'les
   Three Hebrew children in the furnace
   Nevertheless
   Job at the edge of sanity
   Nevertheless
   Peter questioning: "How? Why?"
   Nevertheless
   At my wit's end
   Nevertheless

   The world crashes, burns, mutilates
   Hope says, "Hold on"
   The sky darkens and broods with a dull ache
      like a day-old bruise
   Faith says, "Press on"

"Not my will, but Thine", saith obedience

Nevertheless is steel and brick
    resolution in the face of impossible odds
It is the turning point
    the thick night just before dawn's breaking
I could yet give up
I fail, and He, by all rights, should give up on me
Nevertheless

Daniel 3:16-18 (NIV) "Shadrach, Meshach and Abednego replied to him, 'King Nebuchadnezzar, we do not need to defend ourselves before you in this matter. If we are thrown into the blazing furnace, the God we serve is able to deliver us from it, and he will deliver us from Your Majesty's hand. *But even if he does not*, we want you to know, Your Majesty, that we will not serve your gods or worship the image of gold you have set up.'"

The Way I See It...

Nevertheless can connote a stoic-like giving up, but it need not. I like to think of it as the darkness before the dawn. Less than 200 men at the Alamo, facing certain death, said "nevertheless." Sometimes nevertheless is all that separates us from a life of mere existence, and the one we would like to have. It is not a guarantee of breakthrough, but is almost always the tipping point, after which everything changes.

I have a friend who is Jewish but was never particularly

religious. He always struck me as interested in spiritual things, but we never talked too much about it. Not long ago he reached out to me, knowing I was a pastor. He had questions about Christianity, religion, Jesus, etc. We chatted for a good while off and on over the next few days. He never did come out and overtly profess a faith in Christ, but he had definitely opened the door.

I remember getting the impression from him that he had lived his life a certain way for a very long time but had started to ask himself, "What if there is more to this Jesus?" I can imagine that at that point everything in him wanted to turn back. To give up the fort. I am hoping his tipping point will one day be described as "Nevertheless".

Reaching Out...

God, help me to hold fast, to endure, to have patience, to trust. The only way I can do those things is if you give me the strength to do them. Give me, this day, the strength enough for today. I can do all things through you who strengthen me. Amen.

Reaching In...

1. In what ways are you reminded that God gives you the strength to say "Nevertheless"?
2. Think of a time when you almost gave up, only to have a breakthrough. Did the breakthrough seem like a miracle, or just inevitable in hindsight?

3. Could the story of the three Hebrew children still give us hope if they were *not* saved from the fire?

Day 27: God Is... Not If, but When

Day fades into day
   Time passes, rolls on, blurs into the distance
   Expectations fade and fall away like dead skin
   Hope seems abandoned

Prayers bounce off the ceiling
Like so many BB's
Apathy peers into that life-sucking void
Mocking

Then Hopelessness looks up and discovers
    Not If, but When
On instinct; on his very promise; on his very word

He will act
He will save

He will not leave or forsake
He will give his very best and make all things new

If not today, tomorrow
If not now, someday
Somehow, someway
He will deliver
Not if, but When

Galatians 6:9 (NASB) "And let us not grow weary of doing good, for in due season we will reap, if we do not give up."

The Way I See It...

My first memory is of being about 4 years old, terribly ill in the back seat of a car, my mother and her friend Ozetta rushing me to Texas Children's Hospital (see Day 11). I was suffering from what the doctors called "acute hemolytic anemia", which is a fancy way of saying I had a red blood cell disorder for which there was no real name.

It was only recently that my mother divulged to me that she was sure that I died just as she was carrying me into the emergency room. Years later my brother told me that he and Dad prayed for me that night. I pulled through. Somehow, someway, God broke through.

Fast-forward to when I was about 28 years old, and I had my second brush with death. What British Prime Minister Winston Churchill called his "black dog". This struggle, more existential than actual, was with clinical depression.

It came on me less like a thunderstorm and more like an avalanche. At some point I think I despaired of living. But somehow, someway, God broke through the darkness.

The one thing I learned was that I could not give up. To give up meant that it was over. Cash in your chips. Last one out turn off the lights. I knew that must not happen. And so I declared to God that I would not give up. I would put my head down and push through the blast furnace that was my life. And I would wait for God to show up. One day he did.

I don't take it as a guarantee that he must always show up that way for you or me. But giving up is not an option. Take hold of him, and in due season, somehow, someway, he will show up with deliverance in his wings.

Reaching Out...

God, sometimes I despair. I wonder if I can really get through another day. Give me hope, certitude, and endurance to stay the course. I know you will not give up on me. Neither will I give up. I hold fast to you, knowing you care for me. Amen.

Reaching In...

1. In what ways are you reminded that God will never give up on you?
2. Think of a time you were tempted to give up. What kept you going?
3. Think of a time when you felt far away from God. What brought you near again?

Day 28: God Is... Listener

He hears me
    He hears me when I pray
    When I cry
    When I doubt he recoils not
    When I stand at the door, whether or not I knock
    He hears

    He hears the ache that I fail to put into words
    He knows my ecstasy when promises are fulfilled
    He knows when to speak and when to listen
    When to stand at a distance and when to rush in
    And hold me close

    More than hearing, he perceives
    The earth is his footstool and I sit astride the moon
    Whispering in his waiting ear

as he tilts his head toward my fluttering lips
And furrowed brow
He leans in. And he listens

Isaiah 65:24 (KJV) "And it shall come to pass, that before they call, I will answer; and while they are yet speaking, I will hear."

The Way I See It...

The Mary Baker Eddy Library is a popular tourist destination in Boston's Back Bay area. While living there and going to school, my wife and I visited it to experience their exceptional "Mapparium" globe. It is a unique structure in that it is three stories tall *and* you walk through its center. But, more than that, you can stand anywhere inside, whisper, and anyone else inside the globe will hear it as if you are speaking right into their ear.

Trust me, it is amazing! We were told that this anomaly was only discovered by accident after construction was completed. Pretty cool unplanned benefit, don't you think?

That is how I like to think God hears me when I pray. No matter where in the world I am, no matter what stage of life, every need I have is heard by him as a sweet whisper from a dear loved one. It is comforting to know that I am not a bother to him, nor are you.

I have always wanted to be a parent who hears everything his children say; the dad who knows their heartbeat and is always there. I fail more often than I'd like, but this I know:

God is always listening if you will speak up. Let him know what is troubling you. He loves you.

Reaching Out...

God, I get so busy sometimes that I forget even to pray. I am reminded now that you listen, and you want to hear me unburden myself. Thank you for your attentive ear and your loving way towards me. Help me to have a listening ear to those who need my help as well. Amen.

Reaching In...

1. In what ways are you reminded that God hears you always?
2. Are you humbled by the fact that the God of the universe hears our prayers?
3. What do you do when you feel like your prayers are hitting the ceiling?

Day 29: God Is... The Greatest Story Ever Told

What is he not?
   He is not pulp fiction
   He is not Reader's Digest
   Neither novel nor short story; news column nor missive

He is Wide and Deep. Long and High
Exceeding. Abundant
Above all I could ever think or even imagine

This greatest of stories began primeval
    and is still being told today
It writes itself upon the heart
    and scrawls its love message across the eons
When all seems lost, the story turns a corner once again
    weaving its winsome tale

It is song of songs and ode of odes
It is the book you cannot put down
It is the wondrous story
    of paradise squandered, and bought back

Of ruined lives pulled perilously from the burn pile
Of killers turned by kindness and losers winning life itself
In the greatest story ever told, the hero dies in the end
And yet he lives!

Proverbs 30:5 (KJV) "Every word of God is pure: he is a shield unto them that put their trust in him."

The Way I See It...

I was reading one of my older Bibles the other day, and for some reason I noticed the aroma of its pages. It had the smell of any old book, but I was comforted by it somehow, like the aroma of my dad's Old Spice still unmistakable at the end of a long day, or my grandmother's gardenia perfume lingering in the air of her home.

It is like coming home. At once familiar and inviting, but also holding mysteries. That's how I see God's word, the Bible. It contains the greatest love story ever told, but it never gets old. In fact, every time I read or hear it, it's like experiencing it anew.

We have that same idea about many things in life: that they should be fresh and new as time marches. But most things seldom are. The Bible is one thing that continues to surprise and challenge me, though. God's message of grace from beginning to end is a story that never grows old. On the contrary, the older I get, the more I am amazed and intrigued by the news it delivers. God's story of redemption is truly the greatest story ever told.

Reaching Out...

God, your story inspires me and invites me to continue to reach out to you. Cause me to become more and more a part of your story. I want to be a teller of your greatest story, to be a better bearer of Good News. Help me to have the courage to carry it out with love and grace. Amen.

Reaching In...

1. In what ways are you reminded that God's story is the greatest ever told?
2. What is your favorite book besides the Bible? What about it do you love most?
3. Do you think God's story would be somehow incomplete without you in it? Does that encourage you to reach out to others even more?

Day 30: God is... Not Me (and for that I am grateful)

I am Adam, the blamer
   I am David
      dishonoring God and myself
         in my Bathsheba jaunt
I am Jacob, deceiver, living a life afraid
I am Moses, striking the rock in faithlessness and anger
I am Gideon, asking again and again for a sign
I am Peter, sinking
I am sinner and sufferer
I am guilty, no matter how good

God is Not
God is Good
He is hope when I have run out
He is the summer breeze on a sweltering day

He is the song of redemption
> bursting forth loud and strong

He knows I am dust
> like Adam, and David, and Moses, and…

And in my dusty state I cry out for clear, pure, living water
And it slakes my thirst
Heals my wounded soul
Makes me new
Does everything I cannot do myself
God is not me and for that I am grateful

Isaiah 45:9-10 (CEV) "The clay doesn't ask, 'Why did you make me this way? Where are the handles?' Children don't have the right to demand of their parents, 'What have you done to make us what we are?'"

The Way I See It…

God is God, and we are not–a hard saying, even if we won't admit it. If we are honest, everything in us responds, "Me first!" But also a very helpful and freeing truth: God is God, and I am not, followed closely with God is not ME!

The serpent deceived Eve into thinking that she and Adam could be gods. We still flirt with that belief, even given the admonition and hindsight of Genesis 3. I think it all stems from what I heard through Westminster Theological Seminary once: "One of the greatest lies of the devil is convincing us that God is withholding some good thing from us." But every command, every admonition, every encouragement that sprawls across the pages of God's word is for our good. Even the word goodbye means "God be with ye". You can't mention good without mentioning God!

C.S. Lewis writes in his classic *The Lion, the Witch, and the Wardrobe*:

Mr. Beaver exclaimed, "Aslan is a lion–the Lion, the great Lion."
"Ooh," said Susan. "I'd thought he was a man. Is he quite safe? I shall feel rather nervous about meeting a lion."
"Safe?" said Mr. Beaver. "Who said anything about safe? 'Course he isn't safe. But he's good. He's the King, I tell you."

I once heard a sermon about Nathan's confrontation with David after the Bathsheba affair (2 Samuel 12). We were admonished on how to be like Nathan in the story, calling the King to account. All at once, on my insides, I thought, "But, we are all David!" For some reason, that thought really hit me. We are fellow strugglers, Saints who are sinners.

Letting God be God is a daily struggle. We want to sit on the throne of our own lives, and we want to do it in the lives of others if we can. But it is a dicey thing to stand in judgment of someone; to want to determine outcomes and destiny. Certainly we should care for one another and help when we see someone struggling. But I think David to David is much better, don't you? When we do thusly we are reflecting God's merciful view of us that we are to, in turn, show to others. Letting God be God.

Reaching Out...

God, you are my dear Father, my Savior, all good things to me. Help me not to assume your place in my life or to let anyone else assume that place. There is only one God, and you are him. I trust you to do what is best. You have proven it with your blood. Thank you so much. Amen.

Reaching In...

1. In what ways are you reminded that you are not God?
2. Does it encourage you to see Bible characters more as saints or as sinners?
3. Do you go to God at the moment life abuses you, or do you try to work things out on your own first?

Epilogue

There now, you've done it. A month or so of encouragement completed. I hope your view of who God is has expanded greatly, because who he is can help you to know who you are and who you were meant to be.

Now I challenge you to go back and read it again for another month. Nothing sticks on a simple run-through. You won't lose weight jogging once around the track. You have practiced encouragement for 30 days, and that is a good start. Perhaps as you read through it again this next month some of it will begin to overflow into the world around you.

Take those scripture verses on each day and drill down further into their meaning and context. God wants to show up in your life and to show who He is to you. And he wants to use you to show himself to others as well.

Go show them and tell them who God is.

Appendix

GOD IS...

SMALL GROUP STUDY OUTLINE

Eight Weeks of Spiritual Metaphors and Sanctified Adverbs

In this outline the days of devotion have been categorized into common themes for great discussion for small groups, family devotions, or personal use.

Week 1: God's Timing
God is... Just In Time (Day 2)
God is... Now and Not Yet (Day 5)
God Is... Once And For All (Day 9)
God Is... Not If, but When (Day 27)

Week 2: God's Lavishness
God Is... Treasure Hunter (Day 4)
God Is... Pursuer (Day 20)
God Is... Extravagant (Day 21)

God Is... Gift Giver (Day 15)

Week 3: God's Generosity
God is... Good News (Day 23)
God Is... Good All the Time (Day 16)
God Is... Liberator (Day 22)
God is... Singer Over Me (Day 12)

Week 4: God's Brilliance
God is... Light (Day 1)
God is... My Nightlight (Day 10)
God Is... Burden Lifter (Day 17)
God Is... New Every Morning (Day 19)

Week 5: God's Sovereignty
God is... Turner Of Tides (Day 3)
God Is... Storm Calmer (Day 14)
God Is... Thirst Quencher (Day 6)
God Is... In Control (Day 25)

Week 6: God's Affection
God Is... Home Sweet Home (Day 8)
God Is... Closer than a Brother (Day 18)
God Is... Listener (Day 28)
God Is... Dream Granter (Day 13)

Week 7: God's Resolution
God Is... Nevertheless (Day 26)
God Is...No Regrets (Day 11)

God Is… Not Surprised (Day 7)
God Is… Unseen (Day 24)

Week 8: God's Magnitude
God Is… The Greatest Story Ever Told (Day 29)
God is…Not Me (Day 30)

Made in the USA
San Bernardino, CA
20 April 2015